Where the Waters Know My Name

Vanna
DiCatania

For Caroline.
And for those who did not surface.

Prologue

Water does not announce itself.

It accumulates. It presses. It waits.

What enters it does not remain the same, whether it survives or not.

I

pressure

In Spite of You

You never said the words,
but I heard you loud and clear.
Your actions echoed like cannon fire
through the foreboding halls of my heart–
each move a statement,
each word a lie.
Or was it?

Your silence told the stories
your mouth would not.
Every phrase landed like bricks
on my tired eyes.
Every gesture shifted me
across the board,
your game as tedious
as the life we built.

I realized–too late–
I was only a pawn,
a distraction for your idle hours,
a human stripped of humanity.
You did not see me.
You never knew me.

And yet–
I persisted in spite of your hate.
I grew in spite of your starvation.
I lived in spite of your animosity.

In the end,
you fed me to the fire–
and I walked out burning brighter.

Seduction & Shadow

They learned the map of my quiet–
the small doors I left unlocked at night,
the place behind my ribs where I kept my yes.
They came with the grain of my trust:
a laugh, a helpful hand, a shoulder that smelled of
peppermint.
Sometimes a stranger in a car, crisp with panic;
sometimes the one who folded me into family pictures.
All of them used the same highway: my surprise.

My body unlearned its borders.
A language of flight and freeze moved through my limbs;
my muscles rehearsed a thousand private exits.
There were times I turned bright, mechanical–
a toy on a shelf someone spun and set down,
the edges of me smoothed for someone else's
amusement.
Other nights I kept my fists like secrets,
ready to make a sound I could not recognize as mine.

It was never only one thing:
not always the flash of violence,
but the slow slide of invitation that was really a trap,
the velvet hand that pulled and kept pulling.
It left rooms in me with no furniture,
mirrors that refused to show me the same face.
My respect retreated into the corners,
and with it went my faith in small comforts: a hug, a joke,
a home.

I learned the economy of blame–
how easily it finds me at the till,
how eager people are to count my cost.
I learned to hide the parts of me that tremble,
to make a ledger of what I can explain and what I cannot.
But when the house is quiet I hear the theft again,
the soft arithmetic of someone taking without needing to
ask.
And I am left with the work of putting myself back
together,
with the slow, stubborn labor of naming what was done
and who I am beside it.

Sometimes I am small and furious,
sometimes I am luminous and whole–
both are true and both are mine.
I keep the flashlight under the pillow; I keep a door
cracked,
and in the cracked light I am learning the language of my
own consent,
the syllables of care that begin with me.

After the Water

The ground remembers water
only by the cracks it left behind.
A map of absence,
dust pressed into every seam.

Once, the edges leaned with grasses,
trees stitched shade into the air,
petals loosened their color to the wind.
Now—only husks,
reed shadows brittle in the heat,
stones bleached to silence.

Nothing moves here.
Even sound has gone to ground.
A silence so heavy it erases itself,
a mouth refusing to form a word.

What remains is shape without marrow,
a surface hardened against touch,
emptiness holding its own weight
like a body too tired to rise.

What Remains

The self thins
the way stone yields to water–
a quiet carving,
grain by grain,
until only outline remains.

Masks form before the face,
names cling that never fit.
A hidden core slips beneath the surface,
buried deep,
to survive.

Erosion comes in many shapes:
the sudden strike,
the velvet snare,
each leaving less behind.
Fragments scatter,
mirrors collapse to dust.
Reflection vanishes.

In the absence,
control rises like brittle walls,
but even stone cracks.
Inside the husk–
a silence vast as drought,
an emptiness carrying its own weight.

What remains is shadow without marrow,
silhouette without source,
a vessel waiting
for water that does not return.

Reach

When the light dims
in the corners of the mind,
shadows learn the shape
of your fear.

Smoke moves through the halls.
Thoughts overheat.
Messages cross.

The body understands before language—
lungs tightening,
exits narrowing,
time collapsing inward.

There is no clean escape.
Only the instinct to turn
toward what might hold.

You reach–
not knowing if your hand will be met,
only knowing
you cannot stay where you are.

Through the haze,
through the unsteady geometry of panic,
your voice thins to breath.

Silence presses back.

Still–
the reaching continues.

II

suspension

Wishes

I wish my feelings were stars—
visible, constant, worth navigating by.
But they flicker behind clouds
no one bothers to name.

I wish there were a room in this life
where the walls don't lean in
and whisper, "Not for you."

I wish I could wear my soul like silk,
instead of tucking it behind armor
stitched from silence.

I wish my truth grew like wildflowers—
messy, bright, untamed—
instead of being plucked,
labeled too much.

I wish someone would ask, "Are you okay?"
and want the answer.

I wish I mattered beyond skin and signal—
beyond the weight I carry
and the space I take.

I wish my pain had a curfew,
but it roams like a stray dog
through the alleys of my thoughts.

I wish I didn't speak in cracked glass
or breathe in tones
that make people flinch.

I wish I could wish it all away
like smoke vanishing into wind–
but it clings.

I wish you saw the apology
folded into my eyes,
the understanding I keep writing
in invisible ink.

I wish–

I wish I could whisper these into the night
and have the stars whisper back:

You were never too much–
just too rarely met.

Suspended

A thread trembles,
caught in the lattice of night,
always near the fabric it was meant to join,
never entering, never whole.

Voices brush past without touch.
Boundaries vanish like chalk in the rain.
Desire circles in mute orbits,
its name unsummoned,
its shape half-formed.

Ground gives way beneath the kneeling body—
stone crumbles, dust drifts—
yet the reaching does not end.
Arms extend into absence,
hands cupped for water
that never arrives.

The cosmos is vast and silent,
a frost that answers nothing.
Still the thread hums with yearning,
suspended in its web of stars,
shaping constellations
from what has never been received.

Obsidian Walls

An usurper walks in borrowed flesh,
a faceless steward made of iron law.
It grips the body like reins,
steers with the calm of machinery,
feeds only on necessity.
It cannot hunger,
it cannot weep.

The true heir lingers within—
a flame caught behind obsidian walls,
a bird chained in the hollow of the chest.
She watches through narrow slits of glass,
her cries dissolving into stone.
Every reach is answered
by the cold hand of the warden,
who doles out scraps of touch
as though they were mercy.

From the outside, the automaton thrives:
its face untroubled,
its voice unwavering,
its hands always sure.
The world mistakes this for living,
praises the monster's composure,
and never suspects the silent captive
pressing outward in fire.

Nightfall reveals the cracks:
tears seep like water through fissures,
dreams blaze with unspoken maps of escape.
But dawn reseals the stone,
and the usurper reclaims the helm,
fearless in its dominion.

So the two remain:
the warden without heart,
the prisoner without keys.
One keeps the vessel moving,
the other burns unseen,
a soul paces eternally
inside the fortress of its own flesh.

The Seeing

The hunger is not for touch,
but for vision–
for eyes that do not overlay
the old scripts,
do not fold the body back
into costumes of convenience.

To be seen as unbroken,
as woman, as form,
as self, as flame,
as the shape that has always waited
beneath the masks of survival.

What miracle, this recognition:
a gaze that does not revise,
but restores–
where the body unclenches,
the voice gathers its true timbre,
and every fracture joins again
into wholeness.

Not rewritten, not corrected,
but recognized.
As earth knows water,
as flame knows air–
without explanation,
without disguise.

Should such seeing come,
it will not dazzle with spectacle,
but arrive like dawn on still water:
quiet, certain,
leaving no doubt
true sight is restored.

III

drift

Currents

I have known the weight of an emptying,
where hands reach for me like thirsty roots,
drinking deep, leaving dust in my veins,
where my voice fades in the giving,
spilling, spilling–
until I am a hollowed-out riverbed,
cracked beneath the weight of need.

I have walked among them,
the ones who take and take,
who see kindness as an open tap,
who mistake my stillness for surrender,
who never ask if I have water left to give.

But I have also known the tide that meets me,
the ones who flow as I do,
where I give and am given,
where laughter is an echo, not an effort,
where silence holds no hunger,
only understanding.

With them, I am not drained,
but deepened–
a river fed by another,
currents weaving, circling,
never stealing, only sharing,
never drowning, only rising.

And so I go where the waters know my name,
where the ebb meets the flow,
where reciprocity is not a request,
but a knowing–
a rhythm, a tide, a truth.

Sounding the Waters

At first, the surface shimmered
like something untested–
an edge where water meets stone.

You reached with care,
not plunging, not forcing,
but brushing the air
between gesture and skin.

I received, then remembered,
and memory bit like frost.
I pulled back into the hollow,
and you, steady as tide,
withdrew without storm.

So it went:
ebb and return,
touch and retreat,
a slow rhythm of patience
measured in breaths
and silences.

Distrust was not your burden,
yet you carried it,
lifting it grain by grain
until the weight thinned enough
for me to lean forward,
to risk an unguarded hand
and find it met,
not broken.

At last, the water held.
Not an ocean's crash,
but the quiet certainty
of a pool deep enough to enter–
where trust wavered like ripples,
yet steadied into stillness.

The Quiet

Not silence–
silence is rare, perhaps unreachable–
but quiet.

Quiet in the soft glow of a room,
companions near yet wandering their own distances,
connection steady as breath,
threads that hold without binding.

Quiet in the drift of an afternoon,
sunlight stretched across the floor,
dogs shifting in their sleep,
a weight of comfort pressed into the moment.

Quiet in the first hours of day,
coffee rising like incense,
the world not yet hurried,
even the clamor of birds
woven into a larger calm.

Quiet along the road,
miles unfolding without urgency,
thoughts arriving one by one,
like waves that do not insist—
just come ashore,
then slip away.

Quiet at day's end,
unburdened of labor,
laden with satisfaction,
no need to prove,
no need to seek.

And sometimes—
a quiet of wondering,
what if,
a quiet that carries hope
without direction,
open-handed,
like light across still water.

First Brightness

Somewhere before sound returns,
the air begins to loosen–
not yet warm, only less cold,
as if the dark remembers softness.

A stillness settles in the chest,
its boundaries no longer held in armor,
only uncertain of their shape.
Each breath arrives slower, rounder,
carrying the faint taste of possibility.

From beyond what naming reaches,
a shimmer gathers–
like thought before language,
color before sight,
awareness before light.

It moves toward what has long hidden,
hesitant as touch across a scar,
and the body,
trembling with recognition,
does not retreat.

Within that pause,
something unnamed begins to glow:
a warmth that does not insist,
a light that asks to be met halfway.

Safety and openness lean together,
quietly as dawn folding into itself,
fragile,
but whole enough
to imagine staying.

IV

attunement

Co-play

No words pass between us—
not because there is nothing to say,
but because nothing needs saying.

You move in your rhythm,
and I in mine,
separate orbits,
nested in the same sky.

There's comfort in the shared hush,
the small symphony of being—
a shifting weight, a page turned,
a breath released into stillness.

No asking, no giving,
just the quiet presence
of another life
moving alongside your own.

Here, the silence is not empty.
It is filled
with the soft thrum of trust,
the warmth of nearby gravity,
the joy of simply
being near.

No need to look.
I know you are there.

Beyond the Horizon

Heart drums against the ribs–
a storm of thought raises walls
so high they seem eternal.

Each breath a tightening rope,
each moment a false forever
whispering you cannot pass.

Yet even a black hole ends:
its event horizon lets light escape–
and so do you.

Step, trembling, across.
The storm does not swallow;
it fractures, yields, becomes distance.

On the far side, lungs remember air,
body remembers stillness.
Ground feels strange, unsteady, yet sure;
it holds.

Light is unfamiliar, yet yours.
With every breath the weight dissolves,
silence enlarges–

until only calm remains,
the simple fact
of being here.

Stillness Relearned

The air moves first—
a hush reshaping its weight in the lungs.

Between thought and breath,
a loosened rhythm begins to hold.

Edges blur; the mind stops tracing exits.
Hunger gathers slowly,
not for food, but for return.
Fatigue softens—no longer proof of survival,
only the ordinary ache of being alive.

What once was guarding becomes pulse,
steady, unremarkable, whole—
a presence newly inhabiting its shape.

It reaches quietly,
as warmth meets skin,
as light relearns touch.

The air hums nearer.
Each inhalation less borrowed,
each exhalation less afraid.

No triumph here–only continuity:
a body consenting to stay,
to rest without rehearsal,
to feel and not defend.

Memory opens its hand.
What falls away does not wound–
it simply lands,
weightless,
named enough to be released.

And quiet keeps folding the air,
slow as dusk across water,
until even awareness
forgets to listen,
and the self, unguarded,
breathes without needing to belong.

The Rain Remembers

Rain threads the canopy–
a language older than thought.
Each leaf listens,
translating sound into breath.

Mist gathers the edges of things,
softens bark, fur, feathers, skin.
The body quiets,
settling into air.

Ravens call and answer,
their voices shaping distance.
The forest listens,
each motion echoing another.
Roots drink in silence.
Nothing asks to be allowed–
and still, everything continues.

Breath follows the rhythm of peace,
feet damp with tender earth,
heartbeat keeping time with roots.
Boundaries loosen.
Rain moves without distinction,
through all that lives.

The forest sings itself clean.
Each drop a syllable of forgiveness,
each root lifting the hymn.
Not apart–only quieter,
a shared song the rain remembers.

V

interval

Between the Tides

You are not only what has happened,
nor only what you dream might come.
You are the pause between inhale and exhale,
the ache and the healing that follows.

Each memory returns as a tide,
salted with loss,
bright with reflection.
Each lesson presses against you,
shaping your edges smooth–
not to erase,
but to remind you:
you endure.

Identity is not a verdict.
It is the trembling bridge
between what you carry
and what you release.

Even in the tension,
there is light–
the lantern you keep lit
when everything else is uncertain.
It sways,
but it guides.

Hope is not far off.
It is already in your hands,
woven into the fact
that you are still here,
still becoming.

Inheritance of Water

The ground exhales,
lush with memory.

Water threads between cedar and stone,
finding its own direction—
not fleeing, but redefining.

A gentle step, and the scent rises—
stone, moss, soil, and root.

Breeze slips through open fingers,
steady, unhurried,
a pulse too ancient to name.

Underfoot, the water hums its knowing.
It moves with the patience of roots,
a low song through darkened loam,
carrying the memory of rain
toward the open sky.

Light drifts through misted branches,
touches the surface, warms the skin.

The cedar's breath deepens;
the air tastes green again.
The world remembers how to hold.

The current finds confidence,
broadening with the quiet strength of ease.

Banks lean away;
space opens like trust relearned slowly.

Warmth moves through me
as current through silt–
unforced, inevitable.

The current meets its widening,
salt folding into sweet.

I move until there is no edge–
only the sea,
and the sea keeps moving.

Future Gaze

Light arrives unannounced—
a hush before color,
then gold unspools, slow,
across the water's skin.

Mist parts at its touch,
revealing motion—
the tide's quiet reach,
a tremor widening toward sky.

The air leans into becoming:
seed lifting, wing unfolding—
root tasting morning again.
Breath folds into the rhythm of return.

Brightness gathers, patient,
not to dazzle but to open—
the world tilts forward in its seeing.

And through that widening shimmer,
the horizon breathes,
the day begins its listening,
and I am still becoming.

Continuance

Currents fold through currents,
luminous, alive.
Each particle trembles–
pulsing through bone, through vapor,
through star.
The field widens, revealing itself,
breathing with everything that is.

Author's Note

These poems emerge from a lineage of poets
who listen closely–
to water, to silence, to the body–
and then remain long enough
to let meaning form.

About the Author

Vanna DiCatania—a writer, engineer, and systems thinker whose work explores memory, survival, and the quiet forces that shape identity over time. Her writing often moves through elemental metaphors—water, pressure, accumulation—favoring what is felt and endured over what is declared. She lives in the Pacific Northwest, where rain, silence, and long attention inform both her creative and technical practice. Where the Waters Know My Name is her first published collection.

www.ingramcontent.com/pod-product-compliance
Lightning Source LLC
Chambersburg PA
CBHW051649120626
46551CB00015B/2287